MW00610740

russian aircraft in action

Sukhoi Su-24

Yefim Gordon

POLYGON PRESS

Sukhoi Su-24
© 2003 Yefim Gordon
ISBN 1 932525 01 7

Published by IP Media, Inc.
350 Third Avenue, PMB 368
New York, NY 10010, USA
Tel: 718 305 3355   Fax: 718 305 3356
E-mail: ipmediainc@rcn.com

© 2003 IP Media, Inc.

Design concept and layout
by Polygon-Press Ltd. (Moscow, Russia)
E-mail: info@polygonpress.com

Polygon-Press is an affiliate of IP Media

Printed in Slovakia

All rights reserved. No part of this publication may be repro-
duced, stored in a retrieval system, transmitted in any form or
by any means, electronic, mechanical or photo-copied,
recorded or otherwise, without the written permission of the
publishers.

Contents

This book is illustrated with photos by Yefim Gordon,
Alfred Matusevich and Vyacheslav Martyniuk, as well as
photos from the archives of Yefim Gordon, Simon Watson,
the Sukhoi OKB and *Air Forces Monthly* magazine.

Colour artwork by Sergey Yershov

The author wishes to thank Keith Dexter and Dmitriy
Komissarov for their assistance with the album.

Sukhoi Su–24

In the mid-1960s the tactical arm of the Soviet Air Force (FA) needed a replacement for the elderly Yakovlev Yak-28 *Brewer* tactical bombers. The Yak-28 proved disappointing due to short range and severe restrictions in the use of its weapons. By the mid-1960s, two important factors became evident. The first was the superiority of equivalent US designs, such as the General Dynamics F-111, due to higher performance, wider weapons range and outstandingly superior avionics. The second factor was the rapid development in surface-to-air missile technology; this required new tactical bomber to have supersonic low-level attack capability, which placed high demands on airframe strength and required automatic terrain following capability.

Thus the Sukhoi design bureau (OKB) started work on a tactical bomber which would be the Soviet counterpart of the F-111. Initially the designers settled for mid-set wings with 40° leading-edge sweep. Receiving the in-house designation S-6, it was to have a top speed of 2,500 km/h (1,550 mph) and an all up weight of 20,000 kg (44,090 lb). The two crew members sat in tandem, and the two 7,200-kgp (15,870-lb st) Tumanskiy R-21F-300 afterburning turbojets were placed side-by-side in the rear fuselage, breathing through lateral air intakes.

It soon became evident that a conventional layout was inadequate for the project, and attention was turned to variable-geometry wings and lift-jets, the work proceeding in parallel on these two lines. A completely new project designated **T-6** was started. The first prototype, known as the **T6-1**, entered flight test on 2nd July 1967 with test pilot Vladimir S. Il'yushin at the controls. It had double-delta wings with 60° leading-edge sweep on the inner wings. The crew of two was seated side-by-side. Behind the cockpit were four Kolesov RD36-35 lift engines intended to improve field performance. Initially, two Tumanskiy R-27F2-300 cruise engines rated at 10,200 kgp (22,400 lb st) in full afterburner (again fed by variable lateral air intakes) were fitted; the air for the main engines was used to cool the lift-jets. The intended 11,200-kgp (24,750-lb st) Lyul'ka AL-21F afterburning turbojets were fitted later.

The T6-1 was intended to carry air-to-surface missiles, unguided rockets, air-to-air missiles, bombs and other stores on four wing and two fuselage hardpoints. The wing span was 10.41m (34.14 ft), overall length 23.72 m (77.8 ft), height 6.373 m (20.9 ft) and wing area 45.33 sq.m (487.9 sq. ft). Maximum TOW was 26,100 kg (57,540 lb).

In the course of trials the Soviet Air Force changed its requirements; the ordnance load was increased to such an extent that lift engines were no longer viable. Also, the contradictory requirements of attack at transonic speeds at ground level and short-field capability were still there. Studies by the Central Aero- and Hydrodynamics Institute (TsAGI) showed that variable-geometry wings compared so favourably with every other possible layout that the Sukhoi OKB radically redesigned the T-6 less than six months after the first flight.

The second prototype, designated **T6-2I** (the 'I' denoting *iz**men**yayemaya* [*gheo**metriya*], variable geometry) was completed in late 1969 and took to the air on 17th January 1970, again with Vladimir S. Il'yushin at the controls. The most important change was the new VG wings; they had four sweep settings: 16° for take-off and landing, 35° for loitering and cruise, 45° for manoeuvring and 69° for transonic/supersonic flight. The fuselage was redesigned to increase fuel capacity and the air intakes were modified. The undercarriage was strengthened to let the aircraft carry an increased warload.

Tests of the T6-2I continued until 1976. The aircraft was soon joined by two more prototypes, the T6-3I and T6-4I. The results were encouraging and in December 1971 the bomber entered series production at the Novosibirsk aircraft factory No. 153, receiving the service designa-

tion **Su-24**; the in-house designation at the plant was "*izdeliye* (product) 41". Initial operational capability was achieved in 1973 but it was not until 1975 that the Su-24 was formally included into the inventory. This version was known to the West by the NATO reporting name *Fencer-A*.

Modifications to the design were continually implemented as production progressed. E.g., wing span and wing area were increased soon after the beginning of production. Problems with the variable air intakes caused the intakes to be widened from the 4th production batch onwards (1972) when the to give an increased frontal area. Pressure from the VVS to increase range led the OKB to increase the capacity of the number 1 fuel tank by 1,000 litres (220 Imp. gal.) starting with Batch 8, with a concurrent saving in weight which could be used for extra fuel. Operational experience showed the airframe was strong enough to carry more weapons, so two more hardpoints were added on the centreline, increasing the total to eight and the weapons load to 8,000 kg (17,680 lb). Weapons delivery was controlled by a PNS-24 Tigr navigation/attack system enabling automatic flight along a pre-programmed route, weapons delivery and return to base.

Important changes were introduced in Batch 15 when the shape of the rear fuselage was redesigned to reduce drag. The box-like structure around the engine nozzles was replaced by a more rounded one with a deeply dished bottom between the nozzles and the brake parachute container was moved up. Extensions were added to the fin at the top and along the leading edge; the upper extension supported the A-711 navigation antenna and the leading edge now accommodated the RSDN-10 long-range radio navigation (LORAN) antenna and a cooling air intake for the generators. SPO-15 *Beryoza* (Birch) passive radar warning antennae in triangular fairings were placed on either side of the fin near the top. Other changes made at this time included the addition of leading-edge flaps to the outer wings and a reduction in the number of flap sections from three to two each side. This version was known to the West as the *Fencer-B*. An updated version with Beryoza (Birch) radar homing and warning system (RHAWS) antennae on the air intakes and near the top of the fin was code-named *Fencer-C*.

By 1975 the ongoing problems with the variable air intakes were finally solved by introducing fixed-area intakes from Batch 21 onwards, which also gave a weight saving of 200 kg (440 lb). Aircraft previously built with variable intakes had that control disconnected. As a result, top speed was effectively limited to 1,400 km/h (870 mph) or Mach 1.4 at sea level, except for very short emergency bursts of Mach 2. This was considered an acceptable trade-off against the elimination of previous problems, as 1,400 km/h at S/L had become the standard attack mode. Concurrently the wings were redesigned and given a different airfoil.

Although improvements were constantly incorporated, this did not affect the designation. It was not until 1975 that enough design changes took place to justify a new designation, **T6-M** or **Su-24M** (*modifi **tsee**rovannyy* – modified). The eighth prototype of the Su-24 *sans suffixe* (T6-8) was converted into the Su-24M prototype and redesignated T6-8M, making its first flight on 24th June 1977. Production began in 1978; the aircraft was known at plant No. 153 as *izdeliye* 44; the NATO reporting name was *Fencer-D*.

Major changes were made to the avionics; the most fundamental one was the fitment of a new weapons control system – the PNS-24M Tigr NS. To accommodate the new equipment the forward fuselage was extended by 76 cm and lowered by 15 cm. Apart from the reshaped nose, the Su-24M could be identified by the straight air data boom at the tip of the radome replacing the F-shaped antenna assembly of earlier versions, nicknamed "goose" because of its shape. A Kaïra-24M

(Grebe) day/night low light level TV system/laser designator was fitted, enabling the aircraft to carry laser- and TV-guided missiles and "smart bombs". Also, the number of weapons carried was increased by the addition of a ninth hardpoint.

Combat capability was greatly improved by the addition of an in-flight refuelling system. An L-shaped FPSh-5M retractable IFR probe was installed just ahead of the cockpit to allow refuelling from another Su-24M fitted with a UPAZ-1A Sakhalin "buddy" refuelling pack or an Il'yushin IL-78/IL-78M *Midas* tanker. A new *Karpaty* (Carpathian mountains) defence system was introduced. Rounded boundary layer fences were initially fitted on the edge of the wing glove in line with the inner wing pylons; on some aircraft they housed chaff/flare dispensers. Later, when it was discovered that the wing fences improved longitudinal stability but impaired directional stability, they were removed and the dispensers relocated to the upper rear fuselage.

In the mid-1980s permission was granted to export the Su-24M. In the late 1980s the OKB brought out an export version designated **Su-24MK** (*kommehrcheskiy* – "commercial", i.e., export version) or *izdeliye* 44M. The first flight took place in 1987 and small-scale production commenced in 1988. The Su-24MK differed little from the standard Fencer-D – mainly in the avionics (particularly the IFF system) and weapons options; for example, the Su-24MK could carry more bombs – 38 FAB-100s compared with 34 on the Su-24M and four air-to-air missiles instead of two. All export Su-24MKs had angular wing fences, even though they were being removed at the time from Soviet Air Force Fencers. Sales reported so far are: to Iraq (24), Libya (15), Syria (12) and Iran (9).

In 1978 the OKB started full-scale development of the **T-6MR** reconnaissance version of the Su-24M. Intended as a successor to the outdated and "short-legged" Yak-27R, Yak-28R and MiG-21R, it was to operate at a depth of up to 400 km (250 miles) from the front line, day or night in any weather. The first flight took place in September 1980; two prototypes (the T6MR-26 and T6MR-34) were tested and the aircraft entered production and service as the **Su-24MR** ([*samolyot-*] *razvedchik*, reconnaissance aircraft) or *izdeliye* 48. The NATO code name was *Fencer-E*.

The comprehensive BKR-1 Shtyk (Bayonet) reconnaissance suite included a Shtyk MR-1 synthetic aperture side-looking airborne radar (SLAR) in the nose covering an area of 4 to 28 km (2.5-17.3 miles) from the centreline; a *Zima* (Winter) thermal imager; an Aist-M (Stork-M) TV camera; a Kadr (Photo exposure) PHOTINT system comprising an AP-102 panoramic camera and an AFA-A-100 oblique camera; an Efir-1M (Ether-1M; pronounced *efeer*) radiation monitor in a pod under the starboard outer wing; and a *Tangahzh* (Pitch, in the aeronautical sense) radio monitoring pod or a Shpil'-2M (Spire-2M) laser line-scan pod providing an image of almost photographic quality on the fuselage centreline. Data was recorded on tape but could be instantly transmitted to ground stations if required. Three underfuselage hardpoints and the built-in cannon were removed; two R-60 or R-60M air-to-air missiles could be carried under the port wing for self-defence.

Design work on the **Su-24MP** *Fencer-F* (*izdeliye* 46) electronic countermeasures (ECM) aircraft began in 1976; its mission was electronic reconnaissance and neutralisation of the enemy's air defence radars while escorting attack aircraft to their targets. The two prototypes were converted from Su-24M airframes (the T6M-25 and T6M-35) which were then redesignated T6MP-25 and T6MP-35; the P stands for *postanovschchik pomekh* – ECM platform. (Strictly speaking, the designation ought to have been Su-24PP.) The first flight took place in December 1979. Very little technical information relating to this variant has been released, but it is known to have a sophisticated suite for detecting, locating, analysing, identifying and jamming all known electromagnetic emissions. The bulk of this work is handled by the Landysh

(Lily of the valley) system and the aircraft can carry active jamming pods, such as the Los' (Moose), *Fasol'* (String bean) or *Mimoza* (Mimosette), under the fuselage with no apparent loss of performance. Only about twenty Su-24MPs were reportedly built.

Believe it or not, the Su-24 found peaceful uses as well. In the late 1990s the Flight Research Institute in Zhukovskiy operated two Su-24s – *Fencer-A* "15 White" (c/n 1515301) and Su-24M "11 White" (c/n 1141613) equipped with an air sampling pod for environmental monitoring purposes.

The Su-24 achieved initial operational capability with the Soviet Air Force (VVS) in 1973, even though official acceptance of the type was not given until 1975 – a move not uncommon in the USSR. After being issued to training units, Su-24s were delegated to regiments operating in the Western areas of the USSR and in the Far East. By assigning them to the Ukraine or the Baltic Republics the VVS ensured they could be quickly deployed in times of trouble to Eastern Europe. Later, Su-24 units were stationed in East Germany, Poland and Hungary, but the main Fencer force remained in the USSR.

Among those types displaced from bomber divisions of the Tactical Aviation's Air Armies were the obsolete Il'yushin IL-28 *Beagle* and Yak-28. A division usually included three bomber regiments, each having three squadrons with 10 aircraft per squadron. As production rate grew it was decided to equip some of the fighter-bomber divisions in the 4th, 24th and 30th Air Armies with the Su-24 capable of a more strategic role. These armies had been created in the early 1970s, reporting to the High Command of the Armed Forces to act as a strategic reserve (rather than to Army Fronts or Defence Districts where there was a risk of their aptitude for attacking behind the battle line being wasted in local situations). It was also easier to maintain a tighter control on the use of the nuclear bombs which these aircraft could carry.

On entering service with FA regiments that had previously operated such types as the Yak-28 and MiG-27, the Su-24 proved to be much more demanding in maintenance and service. Considering the complexity of its systems, this was hardly surprising and extra headaches were caused by the fact that this was the Soviet Air Force's first experience with computerised systems.

The Su-24 required appreciably more time and effort to prepare it for a sortie; on average, it needed 45 minutes work by 15 technicians. This effectively doubled ground crew workload per flight – an insupportable situation which was tackled with alacrity. The demands of time could not be reduced because 45 minutes was the minimum time taken to spin up the gyroscopes in the navigation/attack system; some missions requiring a greater degree of accuracy needed as much as 1 hour 20 minutes. Nonetheless, improvements could be made to ease the ground crews' workload.

The biggest headaches to ground and air crews alike came from the avionics. Such was the need for this type of bomber that, as noted earlier, it was rushed into service before the State acceptance trials were completed. The complexity of the many systems and the use of an onboard computer stretched the knowledge and patience of the crews. Malfunctions were frequent and there were cases in the early stages of the Fencer's career when whole squadrons were grounded for several days until remedies were found.

In-flight malfunction of the navigation and targeting system could all too easily put the crew at risk, especially on supersonic nap-of-the-earth (NOE) missions. At best the aircraft was saved but the target missed. It has been known for farms to lose valuable crops, buildings and even livestock when crews failed to realise there was a problem with the equipment and continued the attack in automatic mode, dropping their deadly load on whatever was unlucky enough to be there. There was a case of a crew getting lost, running out of fuel and having to eject because the airmen did not realise in time there was a fault.

The Sukhoi OKB went to great lengths to reduce pre-flight check time by providing easier access to engines, all systems, filters, governors etc. Wheel changing was simplified by eliminating the need for lifting equipment. Special attention was given to the reduction of refuelling time by providing single-point pressure refuelling.

Once the teething troubles had been recognised and acknowledged, they were relatively easy to resolve. One particular cause for satisfaction was the aircraft's ability to withstand bird strikes; a collision with a large eagle and another with seventeen sparrows resulted in no serious damage – at least not to the aircraft.

In spite of these difficulties, he pilots liked the Su-24, affectionately dubbing it "*Chemodahn*" (Suitcase) – an allusion to the slab-sided shape of its fuselage. They appreciated the good field of view, the well-planned flight deck and the automatic flight systems, especially on low-level operations. Flight handling was reasonably easy, even though the Su-24 could be less forgiving in certain circumstances. Slowly but surely the restrictions imposed during the service introduction period were lifted until the Su-24 emerged as a first-rate tactical bomber.

The Su-24 has seen action in several armed conflicts, drawing first blood during the Afghan War where the type made its debut in the spring of 1984. With its weapons load of 7 tons (15,430 lb) – more than double that of other Soviet tactical strike aircraft, its impressive range and sophisticated mission avionics, the Fencer would make a valuable addition to the arsenal of the Soviet contingent helping the pro-Soviet Kabul government fight the Mujahideen rebels. Until then the Su-24 had been unavailable for the war, but the need for such an aircraft was now evident. It was decided to use the type from Soviet bases in Uzbekistan and Turkmenia. Thus, two regiments were seconded to the 40th Army, as the group of Soviet forces in Afghanistan was known. In early April 1984 the 143rd BAP (Bomber Regiment) with 26 Su-24Ms, then based in Georgia at Kopitnari (Kutaisi-1) airbase, was detached to Khanabad – the one in south-eastern Uzbekistan (near Karshi), not the one in Afghanistan. At the same time the 149th GvBAP (Guards Bomber Regiment) with Su-24 *Fencer-Bs* based at Nikolayevka AB in Kazakhstan was relocated to the fighter base at Kokaïdy near Termez, right beside the border.

The primary motive for the presence of Fencers on the Afghan theatre of operations was the need to subdue Ahmad Shah Massoud, the most capable Mujahideen leader. As a rule, the Su-24s were used against area targets such as Mujahideen fortifications. Prior to the sortie, reconnaissance aircraft would photograph the target. Its coordinates would be fed into the bomber's computer, and everything else was largely automatic; the PNS-24 nav/attack system would take the bomber there and drop the bombs. In the 149th GvBAP, Sqn 1 aircraft usually carried four 500-kg bombs each and Sqn 2 and 3 aircraft were armed with twelve 250-kg bombs each; additionally, two drop tanks were always carried.

Su-24 operations in Afghanistan were not very intensive, since the ground forces were more in need of close air support than of carpet bombing. Nor were they particularly successful; the Su-24 had been designed with the relatively flat terrain of Western Europe in mind, and the radar (which could pinpoint small targets such as tanks) had trouble picking out the targets among the jumbled rocks. NOE flying was out of the question because of the many canyons and mountain ridges. Weapons efficiency was low, as guided bombs and missiles showed poor controllability in the rarefied air of the mountains. Bomb-aiming accuracy in level flight was poor; dropping bombs in a 20 to 30-degree dive produced better results but took the bombers within range of the enemy air defences. During the following months, attacks were carried out from altitudes in excess of 5,000 m (16,400 ft) – safely out of range of the Stinger man-portable air defence systems (MANPADS) supplied by the Western Alliance to the rebels.

The next time the *Fencer* appeared in Afghan skies was in 1988. At this stage, when the Soviet Union was already pulling out of the pointless conflict, Su-24 operations were mostly of a psy-war type, intended to exert a constant pressure on the Mujahideen and keep them busy. Sorties were flown not lower than at 7,000 m (22,965 ft) because of the omnipresent Stingers.

Generally the Su-24 had a good reliability record in Afghanistan. The few failures that did take place were mostly associated with hydraulics, flap and engine controls. Initially there were problems with the main nav/attack computer but these were quickly fixed as Afghan experience built up. Sometimes the drop tanks would refuse to give off fuel and had to be jettisoned – which the crews were reluctant to do, knowing that the tanks were in short supply. Because missions were prepared hastily, programming errors occurred and sometimes the navigation data modules would even be installed on the wrong aircraft.

No *Fencers* were lost to enemy fire in the Afghan War. However, there were a few accidents and incidents. On the night of 13th December 1988 a 149th GvBAP forgot to set the wings and flaps for takeoff (they were always rotated to full sweep on the ground to save ramp space) and took off with the wings at maximum sweep. The fully fuelled and bombed-up aircraft managed to get unstuck at the last moment, crashing through the fence around the inner marker beacon and destroying the antenna in so doing; then it climbed away with a shocking 27-degree angle of attack and proceeded to the target. The rest of the sortie went normally, except for the flapless landing on return (the flap control unit had been annihilated when the aircraft hit a fence post). The crew was saved by the bomber's rugged design and the flat terrain around the base (eyewitnesses said the aircraft "could have run all the way to Afghanistan"!).

In December 1988 a 735th BAP Su-24 went off the side of the runway when landing at Khanabad in a stiff crosswind. One of the main gear units hit a pothole and collapsed, rupturing a fuel line and causing a massive fire. The crew escaped but the WSO later died from burns.

Despite the Soviet withdrawal, the Su-24s stayed around for another month, ready to support Najibullah's government if the Mujahideen made an attack on Kabul. In the event, however, this was not needed and the aircraft returned to their home bases in March 1989, ending the *Fencer*'s Afghan involvement.

The type remained in active service in post-Soviet days. Apart from Russia, in the Commonwealth of Independent States (CIS) the Su-24 was operated by the air forces of Azerbaijan, Belarus, Kazakhstan, the Ukraine, Uzbekistan and Tajikistan.

The Russian Su-24s were also actively used in the First Chechen War (1994-96) and the Second Chechen War (1999-2001) against Chechen separatists. These missions did not always go without losses; three *Fencers* were shot down by MANPADS.

It is nearly 35 years since the first flight of the Su-24 prototype and 30 years since it first entered service with the VVS. Despite many improvements to the airframe, avionics and systems, it does not incorporate the latest state-of-the-art and no attempt has been made to render it stealthy. Therefore, plans were in hand to replace it with a modern strike aircraft from the Sukhoi stable – the Su-34 (Su-32FN), a two-seat side-by-side derivative of the Su-27 *Flanker* interceptor. Yet budgetary constraints have caused these plans to be delayed, compelling the Russian Air Force to change its approach. Several Russian companies, such as Gefest&T, are offering mid-life updates for the Su-24M. Designated **Su-24M2**, the first upgraded aircraft having enhanced all-weather/night capability (38 White, c/n 1041643) was unveiled at the MAKS-2001 airshow. No doubt the introduction of the Su-34 will be a high-priority task, but shortage of funds (together with upgrade possibilities) will ensure that the Su-24M and MR will still be in Russian tactical bomber and reconnaissance regiments for a few more years.

Seen here at OKB-51's flight test facility in Zhukovskiy, the T6-1 (the first prototype of the Sukhoi T-6 tactical bomber) differed a lot from subsequent aircraft in the series. This view shows clearly the cranked delta wings similar to those of the Su-15TM interceptor, the separately opening port and staboard canopy halves, the V-shaped window of the laser rangefinder ahead of the windscreen, the engine cooling air intakes on the rear fuselage and the landing/taxi lights on the sides of the nose. The closed dorsal intakes of the buried Kolesov RD36-35 lift jets in the fuselage are not visible here.

The T6-1 lacked a dielectric radome, featuring an all-metal nose ahead of the cockpit windshield.

A "toad's eye view" of the T6-1 seen head-on. Note the shape of the two-dimensional air intakes, the six weapons hardpoints, the straight pitot at the tip of the nose, the back-up pitot near the port wingtip and the nozzles of the lift jets between the underfuselage pylons. The relatively narrow landing gear track is also noteworthy.

A three-quarters rear view of the T6-1, showing the rectangular section of the fuselage forming a box around the engine nozzles, the lack of ventral fins, the brake parachute container at the base of the fin and the radar warning receiver (RWR) antenna near the fin tip. Note the unusual variant of the Soviet Air Force insignia on this aircraft with a pentagon incorporated into the middle of the star.

 After giving up on the use of lift jets which imposed an unacceptable weight penalty the OKB redesigned the T-6 radically, incorporating variable-sweep wings to reconcile speed and field performance requirements. This is one of the prototypes of the Su-24 "sans suffixe" in the assembly shop of OKB-51's experimental plant in Moscow. This view shows clearly the wings at minimum sweep and the double-slotted flaps. Note that the rear fuselage, which was detachable for engine maintenance/change, is still unpainted, indicating that the aircraft is undergoing conversion to a new variant (probably the Fencer-B prototype). The aircraft in the background is the T10-1, the first prototype of the Su-27 fighter (NATO code name Flanker-A).

The T6-2I (coded 62 Yellow) at the flight test facility during manufacturer's tests. Note the warning markings near the radome ("Danger, HF radiation") and the air intake bodies ("Danger, jet intake"). Note also the Sukhoi OKB's "winged archer" logo beneath the cockpit and the red band near the top of the fin. The landing lights are still built into the forward fuselage sides. The all-movable stabilizers "bled" down to maximum nose-down position when hydraulic pressure fell off after engine shutdown.

The T6-2I at the Flight Research Institute (LII) airfield in Zhukovskiy. All six hardpoints are equipped with MBD3-U6-68 multiple ejector racks carrying 250-kg (551-lb) FAB-250 bombs. Due to take-off weight limitations the two MERs under the fuselage carry five bombs each instead of six; the total number of bombs is 34, equalling a warload of 8.5 tons (18,740 lb). Note the colour of the radome, the different Sukhoi OKB badge, three test mission markers and cruciform photo calibration markings beneath the cockpit and the blue fin stripe replacing the earlier red one. An ILS aerial is mounted above the air data boom carrying pitch and yaw sensor vanes.

One more view of the fully loaded T6-2I at Zhukovskiy with wings at maximum sweep. As is the case with some Western strike aircraft, the pylons under the Su-24's outer wings rotate as wing sweep chages, remaining parallel to the fuselage centreline. This view shows well the intakes' boundary layer splitter plates.

One of the Su-24 prototypes with the wings at minimum sweep. The aircraft carries 24 FAB-250s on MERs on the wing pylons and a pair of 500-kg (1,102-lb) FAB-500s on the fuselage stations, which equals an ordnance load of 7 tons (15,430 lb).

The sixth prototype Su-24 (T6-6) was coded 66 Yellow. Here the aircraft is armed with SPPU-6 gun pods with depressable six-barrel 23-mm Gatling machine guns (here with the barrels at the maximum deflection of 45°) on the inner wing pylons, OFAB-250ShN low-drag bombs for low-level strike on the fuselage stations and Kh-23 rockets on the outer wing pylons. The T6-6I still had a straight air data boom with an ILS aerial above it and nose-mounted landing lights (they were moved to the wing roots on production aircraft); the fin top band was white.

Two views of the T6-27 (coded 27 White), another Fencer-B development aircraft, carrying three Kh-29 rockets on the inner wing and centreline pylons plus two Kh-23 rockets on the outer wing pylons. The red colour of the rockets identifies them as inert rounds for initial weapons trials; note the photo calibration markings on the rear fuselage. The wing fences were a recent addition at the time the pictures were taken - they have not been painted yet!

24 Blue, a Su-24 "sans suffixe" representing the second production version known in the West as the Fencer-B. This view illustrates some of its features - the kinked forward segment of the nose gear doors consisting of two hinged parts, the faired heat exchanger on top of the centre fuselage and the antenna faired into the fin leading edge with a cooling air intake below it. Production Su-24s featured a so-called "goose" - an L-shaped strut at the tip of the radome mounting an antenna array; the radome itself was white. Note also the faired electronic countermeasures (ECM) antennas on the air intakes and the sides of the fin near the top and the boundary layer fences forming extensions of the inner wing pylons.

The T6-8M, the prototype of the Su-24M (NATO code name Fencer-D), at the LII airfield in Zhukovskiy in original guise. Note the extended nose, the extended wing leading edge root ECM fairings, the non-standard twin nose gear doors which remain open when the gear is down, the patch of bare metal and the absence of sensors on the underside of the nose where modifications have been made, the modified fin leading edge and the photo calibration markings on the fuselage. Despite the redesigned nose, the aircraft retains the "goose" typical of the initial-production Su-24 (compare this to the production aircraft on the opposite page).

The T6-8M at a later stage of the trials wearing an unusual three-tone camouflage and the Sukhoi OKB "winged archer" badge beneath the cockpit. The sensor array under the nose has been reinstated. The aircraft carried no tactical code.

Another view of the camouflaged T6-8M, showing the shape of the rear fuselage around the engine nozzles and the ventral fuel jettison pipes under the nozzles. These features are identical to the final production version of the Su-24 «sans suffixe» (Fencer-C).

▲
An early-production Su-24M coded «07 White». Note the long straight air data probe at the tip of the radome and the wing fences (making the NATO reporting name Fencer oddly appropriate). The port canopy half is secured by a retaining rod to keep it from slamming down on somebody's head or hands when there is no pressure in the hydraulic system.

Another view of Su-24M "07 White", showing the characteristic profile of the nose radome. Production Su-24s and Su-24Ms were normally painted light grey overall with white undersurfaces.

▶

Two views of Su-24s parked on a rain-lashed hardstand at Ostrov airbase near Pskov, north-western Russia. The base, whose name means "island" in Russian, hosts the Russian Navy's Combat and Conversion Training Centre (i.e., operational conversion unit).

The examples in these photos are representative of the very first production version known as the Fencer-A, as indicated by the boxy structure around the engine nozzles and the placement of the brake parachute container very close to the nozzles. Oddly, the starboard airbrake-cum-mainwheel-well-door is open on all aircraft in the lineup while the port one is closed, as it should be on the ground. Note the fuel jettison pipe between the engine nozzles.

Su-24 "29 White" seen at Ostrov AB in 1998 is an example of the penultimate version of the Su-24 "sans suffixe" called Fencer-B in NATO parlance. Note the 3,000-litre (660 Imp. gal.) PTB-3000 drop tank suspended on the centreline pylon.

A trio of Fencer-As at Ostrov AB; note the different location and smaller size of the yellow radiation and air intake warning triangles. While the aircraft are in flyable storage, the resident Fencer-As were awaiting retirement and disposal on site.

Su-24 "05 White" is an example of the final variant of the Su-24 "sans suffixe" known as the Fencer-C. Theis version can be identified by the ECM antenna fairings on the air intake bodies and the fin sides.

▲
Another view of Su-24s with PTB-3000 drop tanks under the wings in storage at Ostrov AB in 1998. The incredible fact that two neighbouring Fencer-As in the line-up carry the same tactical code, 29 White (quite apart from the Fencer-B shown on the preceding page!), is explained by the fact that the Su-24s were ferried to Ostrov for storage from various units and all three bombers obviously belonged to different regiments.

PTB-3000 drop tanks lying in a neat row on the edge of the hardstand. These huge tanks were used for both ferry flights and long-range operations.
▶

Close-up of the PTB-3000 on the centre-line hardpoint of Fencer-B "29 White". The fins were set at more than 90° in order to provide adequate clearance between tank and wing/fuselage. Typically of the Soviet/Russian Air Force, drop tanks and such were marked with the aircraft's tactical code to stop them from being stolen and used on another aircraft – but clearly that did not always help; this drop tank comes from a sister ship coded 23! The yellow rectangles on the fuselage carry maintenance stencils.
◀

Front view of Su-24 Fencer-B "29 White". The canopy is closed by a heavy canvas cover which protects the Perspex from the ultraviolet radiation of the sun, delaying the appeerance of micro-cracks which generate annoying reflections (this phenomenon is known as "silvering").

The tails of these Fencer-As show how the Su-24's rudder is cut away from below, with a radar warning receiver aerial at the base. On later versions the space between it and the fuselage was occupied by the brake parachute container which was moved up considerably.

Another view of the Fencer-A lineup at Ostrov AB. Left to right: 26 White, 29 White No. 1, 29 White No. 2 (ex 43 White), 24 White and 74 Red.

The Su-24's wings were moved aft into fully swept position after landing to save space on the hardstand. This view shows the Su-24's large spoilers used for roll control.

On this Su-24 the nose radome has been draped in a canvas cover, too – but little good did it do because the canvas is coming apart.

This Fencer-A (52 White) at Ostrov AB has had the entire forward fuselage wrapped in tarpaulins. The wraps bear the aircraft's tactical code on a black circle. The aircraft is a late-production example, as indicated by the dorsal heat exchanger fairing usually found on later variants.

As the wings are moved back into maximum sweep position the centre of gravity shifts aft, causing the Su-24 to assume a nose-up position. Fortunately, unlike some variable-geometry aircraft, even an unladen Fencer does not exhibit a tendency to tip over on its tail in this situation.

This Fencer-C undergoing maintenance has had a support placed under the tail – just in case. All wheel well doors are fully open. Note that skin panels mounting the centre portions of the ventral fins have been removed for access to some of the equipment in the rear fuselage.

Fencer-A "26 White" at Ostrov AB. The slope behind it faced with concrete slabs functions both as a revetment wall and as a jet blast deflector, allowing the engines to be run after the aircraft has been aligned with the taxiway.

This late-production Fencer-A (note heat exchanger) operated by the Russian Navy's Black Sea Fleet is rather more fortunate. When this picture was taken in 1998 it was fully operational and based at Gvardeyskoye AB in the Crimea which the Ukraine has leased to the Russian Naval Air Arm. Note the generally better surface finish on this aircraft and the different design of the nosewheel mudguard. It is hard to say why a car tire has been place on top of the aircraft. The vehicle in the background is an APA-5 ground power unit on a Ural-375D truck chassis.

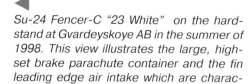

Su-24 Fencer-C "23 White" on the hard-stand at Gvardeyskoye AB in the summer of 1998. This view illustrates the large, high-set brake parachute container and the fin leading edge air intake which are characteristic of the Fencer-B/C.

Front view of a Fencer-C at Gvardeyskoye. The pilot's PPV head-up display (HUD) is visible through the windshield.

Preparations are in hand for another day's flying training over the Black Sea as a gaggle of Su-24s basks in the sun at Gvardeyskoye AB. The nearest aircraft is provided not with the usual tarpaulin but with a modern cockpit cover made of reflective metallised fabric which also keeps the cockpit from turning into a steam bath in the summer season.

▲ Gvardeyskoye AB is a large and well-equipped base with a large flight line boasting an excellent surface and a concrete-lined jet blast deflector. In post-Soviet days, however, it was not much used, and the arrival of the Russian Fencers (the Ukraine operates the type, too) was a welcome spell of activity. Note the bicycle leaned against the aircraft; servicemen cycling around CIS airbases are a pretty common sight. Small wonder, as legging it around the place can get quite tiresome.

Fencer-Cs "23 White", "01 White" and "21 White" await the next sortie. Note the drop tank resting on a wooden cradle next to the latter aircraft. ▼

Fencer-B "28 White" (c/n 1715324) at Gvardeyskoye AB. The Fencer-B differs from the late-model 'A in having ECM fairings on the air intake bodies and tail. Note the tactical code and c/n on the air intake covers. ▶

▲
Su-24s «01 White», «21 White» and «07 White» in the maintenance area at Gvardeyskoye AB. The second aircraft is unserviceable, being minus the port engine.

Another angle on the maintenance ramp, with a fourth aircraft («27 White») on the left. Note the trestle under the tail of Fencer-B «21 White». Fencer-Cs «01 White» and «27 White» are obviously recoded, the tactical code being applied over a blotch of darker paint.
▶

◀
Three-quarters front view of Fencer-C «27 White» (c/n 2315337). Note the "clip-on" ladders. Built-in boarding steps were generally rare on Soviet combat aircraft..

A line-up of seven Fencer-Cs ready for action at Gvardeyskoye, including «10 White», «11 White», «09 White», «12 White» and «17 White».
◀

▲
Fencer-C "28 White" (c/n 1715324) differs slightly in the design of the «goose» and undernose aerial from «27 White» on page 26. Interestingly, the port air intake cover comes from another example coded «26 White» (c/n 2215334).

A trailer-mounted ground power unit stands beside Fencer-C «01 White» to provide electric power during maintenance.

▶

Many operational Su-24s show considerable signs of wear and tear, as exemplified by Fencer-C «27 White» at Gvardeyskoye. Note the unit badge beneath the windscreen. Again, the aircraft is obviously recoded, the part of the intake body with the tactical code making a marked contrast with the rest of the weather-stained airframe.

A pair of Su-24Ms coded «53 Red» and «57 Red» makes a banked turn over the Volga River near Akhtoobinsk, seat of the Air Force Research Institute. The camera ship is a slow transport, so the bombers fly with the wings at 16° to keep formation.

This view of a Su-24M shows that the wing and stabilator leading edges are parallel when the wings are at 69° maximum sweep. The radome on this particular example is unspeakably dirty, and more dirt emanates from the wing glove fairings near the wing pivots. The retractable FPSh-5M refuelling probe is positioned on the centreline ahead of the windscreen. Note the white colouring of the wing/stabilator leading edges and the offset position of the dorsal heat exchanger.

Su-24M «67 White» parked at the Russian Navy Combat and Conversion Training Centre, Ostrov AB. Note the red covers on the dipole aerial aft of the cockpit and the hemispherical sensor of the Mak-UFM missile warning sensor further aft.

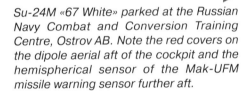

Two more Su-24Ms, «64 White» and «68 White», under wraps at the Russian Navy Combat and Conversion Training Centre. Unlike the Fencer-As depicted earlier, these aircraft are not in storage but are actually based at Ostrov and belong to the 240th GvOSAP (Guards Independent Composite Air Regiment).

Su-24M «66 White» is one of the Fencer-Ds belonging to the Russian Navy Combat and Conversion Training Centre. This example carries an L-080 Fantasmagoriya-A (Phantasm-A) electronic reconnaissance (ELINT) pod on the centreline pylon.

Three more views of Su-24Ms «64 White» and «68 White». The main gear doors are fully open. Note the kinked nose gear door consisting of two parts, a characteristic feature of the Su-24M, and the curvature of the colour division line across the wing fences. Note that the tactical code is repeated on the «pig snout» plate at the tip of the nose pitot cover.

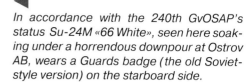

In accordance with the 240th GvOSAP's status Su-24M «66 White», seen here soaking under a horrendous downpour at Ostrov AB, wears a Guards badge (the old Soviet-style version) on the starboard side.

A close-up of the «candy bar» shaped L-080 ELINT pod on Su-24M «66 White». The front and rear portions are dielectric.

▲
Head-on view of a very late-production Fencer-D coded «94 Blue» (c/n 1241613), another 239th TsPAT machine.

This late Fencer-D, a Batch 10 aircraft (c/n 1041611?) belonging to the 239th TsPAT (Aviation Hardware Demonstration Centre) at Kubinka AB, represents the export version designated Su-24MK. The blue tactical code is noteworthy, but the dark green/ dark earth tactical camouflage with pale blue undersurfaces similar to the one worn by Iraqi Air Force examples is even more unusual for a Russian Air Force Su-24. Note the lack of wing fences on this aircraft.

◄
◄

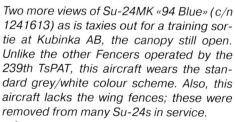

«94 Blue» is prepared for a mission amid a jumble of ground support equipment that comes with other Su-24s. Note the packed brake parachutes on the left.

239th TsPAT Su-24MKs await the next sortie. The Su-24 hardstand at Kubinka is well equipped, with an energy supply system obviating the need for mobile ground power units.

Two more views of Su-24MK «94 Blue» (c/n 1241613) as is taxies out for a training sortie at Kubinka AB, the canopy still open. Unlike the other Fencers operated by the 239th TsPAT, this aircraft wears the standard grey/white colour scheme. Also, this aircraft lacks the wing fences; these were removed from many Su-24s in service.

«93 Blue», another camouflaged 239th TsPAT Su-24MK (c/n 1041623), taxies out for a training sortie. The aircraft is armed with S-25-OF heavy unguided rockets on the wing glove pylons and R-73 air-to-air missiles on the outer wing pylons. The «wet» centreline pylon mounts an UPAZ-1A Sakhalin «buddy» refuelling pod allowing the Su-24 to refuel other tactical aircraft. The angular wing fences of «93 Blue» house APP-50 chaff/flare dispensers.

«94 Blue» is prepared for engine starting, using an APA-5D GPU in this instance; the brake parachute pack lies beside, ready for loading. The APA-5's lateral cable booms swing out to the sides, allowing the vehicle to power up two aircraft at a time

«92 Blue», the second of three camouflaged Su-24MKs operated by the 239th
TsPAT, fires up its Lyul'ka AL-21F afterburning turbofans at Kubinka on a bleak winter's
day. The aircraft shows signs of operational
wear and tear, with weathered areas on the
forward fuselage side touched up in fresher
blue paint.

«92 Blue» taxies out, showing the steel
plates protecting the inboard portions of
the wing flaps from damage when they slide
inside the wing gloves as wing sweep is
changed.

▲
Due to the unit's «showcase» nature the Su-24MKs at Kubinka AB were frequently displayed to various visiting military delegations and at open doors days. In the upper photo «91 Blue» is seen together with a Su-25 of the Nebesnyye Goosary (Celestial Hussars) display team which was disbanded soon afterwards.

▼

Two more views of Su-24MK «91 Blue» during displays at Kubinka. The aircraft is fitted with six MBD3-U6-68 MERs (two of them in tandem on the centreline) carrying a total of 36 FAB-250 bombs (blue-painted inert ones) weighing 9,000 kg (19,840 lb).

▶
▶

◀◀ ▲▲
Su-24M «11 White» (c/n 1141613) belonging to the Sukhoi OKB performs a simulated refuelling of Su-30 «597 White» (c/n 79371010101) belonging to the Ispytateli (Celestial Hussars) display team of the Flight Research Institute during the MAKS-97 airshow.

Su-24M «11 White» taxies in at Zhukovskiy after the demo fligh, wings already at full sweep. The UPAZ-1A refuelling pod can be seen under the belly.

◀

◄ Su-24MK «93 Blue» (c/n 1041623) refuels a sister aircraft coded «91 Blue» during an open doors day at Kubinka AB.

Two Su-24Ms can take on fuel simultaneously from an IL-78 tanker, as demonstrated by Fencer-Ds «17 White» and «19 White» formating with IL-78M «30 Blue» over Kubinka AB. ▼

Another view of a pair of Su-24MKs in «buddy-buddy» refuelling formation. ▶

Su-24M «45 Red» is one of several operated by the 968th IISAP (Instructional & Test Composite Air Regiment) which is part of the Russian Air Force's 4th TsBP i PLS (Combat and Conversion Training Centre) in Lipetsk. Note the unit badge and the five mission markers on the nose applied to mark successful live weapons training sorties.

Su-24M «42 Red» is prepared for the day's flying at Lipetsk AB. Like the other resident Fencers, the aircraft has been recoded. The GPU in this case is an APA-5DM based on a diesel-powered Ural-4320.

«41 Red», another 968th IISAP Su-24M (seen here sharing the ramp at Lipetsk with a Mikoyan MiG-29), wears 14 mission markers. It is equipped with a UPAZ-1A refuelling pod.

▲
Su-24M «41 Red» features APP-50 chaff/flare dispensers on the upper side of the rear fuselage to enhance the aircraft's protection against heat-seeking missiles (see also page 44).

Another view of the flight line at Lipetsk.

Su-24Ms lined up under threatening skies at Lipetsk. Note the open brake parachute container clamshell doors on «47 Red».
◄

◄

Interestingly, none of the 4th Combat and Conversion Training Centre's Su-24Ms has the tactical code repeated on the fin, as is customary in the Russian Air Force. On the other hand, the tactical code is repeated on the nose gear door, which is certainly unusual.

Su-24M «40 Red» sports four mission markers.

The flight line in Lipetsk is equipped with removable jet blast deflectors made of steel. This type of structure is more common at Soviet/CIS airbases than the «built-in» version of the kind seen at Ostrov AB.

Although the Su-24M's entire nose ahead of the windshield is painted white, not all of it is dielectric. Here the extent of the actual radome is clearly visible, as the special radio-transparent white paint used on dielectric fairings has become so weathered as to turn a dirty grey colour.

▲
This view of a Su-24M shows the wings at minimum sweep, the high-lift devices (slotted flaps and leading-edge slats) and the four underfuselage hardpoints (two in tandem and two side by side). The foremost pylon and the two side-by-side pylons are fitted in this case. The airbrakes/main gear doors are just about to close as the aircraft «cleans up» after take-off.

Su-24M «44 Red» «burns rubber» at the moment of touchdown in Lipetsk. This is one of several Fencer-Ds upgraded by the Russian avionics/weapons integrator Gefest & T. The mid-life update can be identified by the faired chaff-flare dispensers on top of the aft fuselage; the fairings have small air intakes at the front. The aircraft carries RBK-500 cluster bombs on the centreline pylons.

▶

Close-up of the Gefest & T logo on the air intake of Su-24M «40 Red», another example upgraded by the company. Note the «cross-hairs» in the middle of the Cyrillic letter F.

The Su-24Ms of the 4th TsBP i PLS are by far the most actively flying Fencers in Russia, surpassing even those the naval examples based at Ostrov AB.

The Su-24Ms of the 968th IISAP wear a badge depicting a rampant bull with the word «Vseg**da**» («always» in Russian). The badge signifies readiness to take on any adversary, anytime, anywhere (equvalent to the «Semper paratus» motto of some Western squadrons). A more unofficial interpretation is «we'll have everybody, everywhere, every time and in every possible way».

«45 Red», yet another 4th TsBP i PLS Su-24M which had undergone a mid-life update by Gefest & T, lands at Ostrov AB. The weatherede radome is well visible. ▼

▲ ▶

Su-24Ms «45 Red», «46 Red» and «40 Red» make a smoky flypast in echelon starboard formation. All three aircraft carry small bombs on the centreline; a minimum ordnance load is enough for weapons training.

▲
The Su-24M served as a basis for the Su-24MR Fencer-E reconnaissance aircraft. This head-on view shows the reconnaissance version's characteristic asymmetric external stores arrangement with a Efir-1M electronic intelligence (ELINT) pod on the starboard wing pylon and a dual missile rack with two R-60 AAMs for self-defence under the port wing.

The Su-24MR has a much smaller nose radome, as revealed by the discolouration of the dielectric parts on the T6MR-1 prototype («26 White») converted from a Fencer-A (c/n 0115305). The space aft of it is occupied by a Shtyk MR-1 side-looking aircraft radar (SLAR) with elongated flush dielectric panels. The prototype lacked the IFR probe of production examples.

The nose of the Su-24MR is painted white right up to the windshield, just as on the regular Fencer-D, in order to conceal its special nature from the adversary's aerial reconnaissance and space surveillance assets. This example coded «15 White» carries an Shpil'-2M laser line-scan pod on the centreline pylon. The white «hump» on the dorsal heat exchanger fairing is not a cap of snow but a dielectric panel. Note that the drop tanks apparently come from another aircraft; even writing the tactical code in really huge digits does not help!

Su-24MR «12 White», seen here at the moment of rotation, carries a large photo reconnaissance/ELINT pod on the centre-line pylon.

▲
This Su-24MR coded «40 Yellow» (c/n 0941648) is used as a demonstrator by the Sukhoi Design Bureau and based in Zhukovskiy, hence the flashy colour scheme in the Russian flag colours of fhite, blue and red. Here the aircraft is fitted with a PHOTINT/ELINT pod; the open camera port is visible here.

Su-24MR c/n 0941648 in the static park of MosAeroShow-92. In this instance it carries an Shpil'-2M pod; this near head-on persoective illustrates the pod's elliptical cross-section. Note that the AAM adapter under the starboard wing is the wrong one, i.e., it is intended for the starboard side (the upper missile should be on the outer side!).

▶

This view of the Su-24MR demonstrator at MosAeroShow-92 shows to advantage the special colour scheme. ▶

The tail unit of Su-24M «40 Yellow». ▶

Close-up of the Shpil'-2M laser line-scan pod on the centreline station of Su-24M «40 Yellow». ▶

 Su-24MR «40 Yellow» (c/n 0941648) – this time with no external stores – takes off from Zhukovskiy's runway 12 for a demonstration flight during one of the MAKS airshows.

«40 Yellow» completes its landing roll on runway 30 at Zhukovskiy. The aircraft is a regular participant of the flying programme during Moscow airshows.

Su-24MR «40 Yellow» passes in front of the crowd. Note the Vee shape of the colour division lines on the underside and the dirty marks sloping downwards from the stabilator pivots (a result of the stabilators' habit of «bleeding» down to maximum deflection when the engines are inoperative).

The other special mission derivative of the Su-24M was the Su-24MP Fencer-F electronic countermeasures aircraft. This view shows the square-shaped dielectric panels on the sides of the nose (hiding jammer antennas), the characteristic ECM aerials under the nose and on the air intakes, and the centreline Fasol' jammer pod.

The few Su-24MPs were stationed in the Far East and the Ukraine (the latter aircraft were retained by the newly-independent Ukraine after the break-up of the Soviet Union). Here, a Russian Air Force Su-24MP in wraps sits on a snowbound ramp at Lipetsk. Note that the outer wings are wrapped up, too.

This 4th TsBP i PLS Su-24MP coded «15 White» is apparently due to awaken from winter sleep and make a training flight; mechanics are about to remove the canvas covers from the airframe.

«15 White», a Ukrainian Air Force Su-24MP, sits in front of a hardened aircraft shelter (HAS) at Chortkov AB. The immaculate finish on this aircraft is noteworthy.

▲
Another view of ukrainian AF Su-24MP «15 White». The nose gear doors are open for maintenance. The 118th OAPREB (Independent ECM Regiment) at Chortkov operating the type transitioned to the Su-24MP from the Yakovlev Yak-28PP.

As is the case with the Su-24MR, the nose of the Su-24MP is painted entirely white to disguise its role and hopefully prevent its from being specially chosen as a target.

This Ukrainian Air Force Su-24M coded «19 White» carries UAF roundels on the forward fuselage (which makes an interesting comparison with the aircraft on the opposite page) and dragon artwork. Note the L-080 Fanmtasmagoriya-A ELINT pod on the centreline station.

Ukrainian Air Force Su-24 Fencer-B «49 White» (c/n 1615324) undergoing maintenance at its home base, Chortkov AB. The radome swings open to port, revealing the two antenna dishes; the larger one is for the Puma fire control radar while the small one underneath is for the terrain following radar.

 Two more views of Ukrainian Air Force Su-24 «49 White» (c/n 1615324) unbuttoned for maintenance, showing the positioning of the UAF roundels on the wings and the removable panels on the upper fuselage for access to the control runs and other systems.

The nighbouring aircraft coded «50 White» is also being worked upon. The drop tank is inscribed «50 starboard» but the «5» has almost vanished – though it is hard to say why.

The Ukrainian Air Force also managed to keep some Fencer-As flying, as illustrated by «65 White» here. Note the variance in the shield-and-trident tail insignia on individual aircraft; the crudely overpainted red star is showing from under the UAF insignia on this one. The panels carrying the middle portions of the ventral fins are removed, showing that «65 White» is a bit unairworthy for the time being.

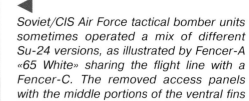

Soviet/CIS Air Force tactical bomber units sometimes operated a mix of different Su-24 versions, as illustrated by Fencer-A «65 White» sharing the flight line with a Fencer-C. The removed access panels with the middle portions of the ventral fins are lying behind the aircraft.

Portside view of Su-24 «49 White» with the radome open. Note the wooden cradles for the drop tanks.

The Ukrainian bases where the Su-24s are stationed feature earthen revetments.

The Islamic Republic of Iran Air Force (IRIAF) was one of the few export customers for the Su-24. Apart from the Su-24MKs delivered directly from Russia, the IRIAF retained several ex-Iraqi examples which sought shelter in neutral Iran at the closing stage of the 1991 Gulf War. Here, IRIAF Su-24MKs serialled 3-6853 (above) and 3-3810 (right) are seen at military hardware exhibitions at Teheran International airport.

Two IRIAF Su-24MK (3-6807 and 3-6811) cruise over the snow-covered mountains of northern Iran. These photos illustrate the two-tone camouflage worn by export Fencers.

▲
The rear fuselage and tail unit of the Fencer-A, the first production version of the Su-24, showing the low-set brake parachute container. This particular aircraft serving as a ground instructional airframe at the Ukrainian Air Force Technical School near Kiev is the T6-19 development aircraft («619 White»; c/n 0215307?). Note the photo calibration marking on the tail.

This view clearly illustrates the difference in rear end treatment between the Fencer-A (background) and the Fencer-C. Note the antenna and cooling air intake built into the latter aircraft's fin leading edge.

▶

▲
The rear fuselage and tail unit of the Su-24M (illustrated here by 239th TsPAT «92 Blue»), except for the shorter, upward-curved fuel jettison pipes.

Close-up of the Su-24M's brake parachute container, with the radar homing and warning system (RHAWS) antenna array above
◄

▲
The Su-24 has four underwing hardpoints. This particular example features non-standard wing glove pylons allowing two stores to be carried on each inboard station.

The outer wing pylons rotate as wing sweep changes, remaining parallel to the fuselage axis. This aircraft carries 32-round UB-32 rocket pods for firing 57-mm S-5 folding-fin aircraft rockets (FFARs).

▼

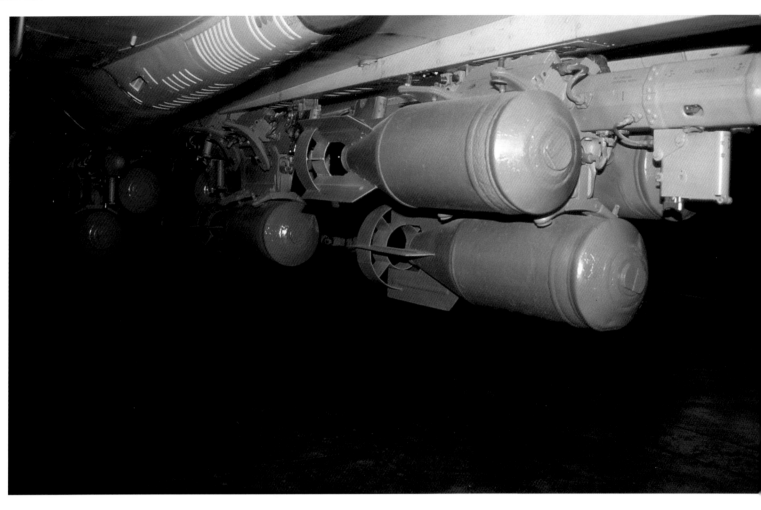

◀ ▲

MBD3-U6-68 multiple ejector racks can be carried on any of the Su-24's hardpoints. Up to six of these MERs can be fitted at a time for carrying FAB-250 HE bombs. The starboard one of the two elongated ventral fairings visible in the left photo houses a 30-mm Gryazev/Shipoonov GSh-6-30 six-barrel Gatling cannon; the muzzle opening is closed by «eyelid» shutters.

Double launcher adapters for R-73 air-to-air missiles can be carried on the outer wing pylons. These are usually fitted to the Su-24MR (here, «40 Yellow», c/n 0941648) and Su-24MP.

▶

The generator cooling air intake at the base of the fin is a feature of the Fencer-B and subsequent versions.

The dorsal heat exhanger for cooling the mission avionics was introduced on the final batches of the Fencer-A.

The Su-24's hefty wing pivot box is manufactured as a singe whole with the fuselage. This is the port wing pivot and the riveted structure around it. Note the shallos strake which organses the airflow around the wing/fuselage joint.

Another view of the Su-24's wing pivot. ▶

Up to three 3,000-litre (660 Imp. gal.) PTB-3000 drop tanks can be carried on the fuselage and inner wing hardpoints. Small canards with negative incidence are fitted at the front to facilitate separation when the tank is jettisoned. ▼

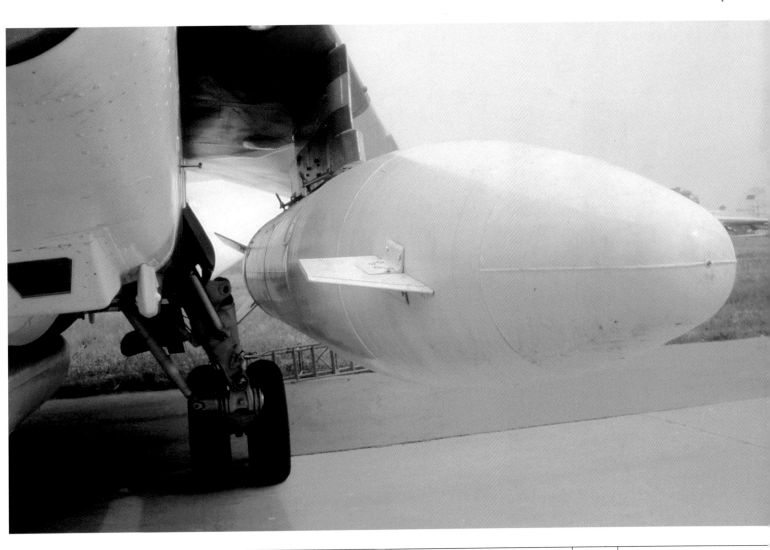

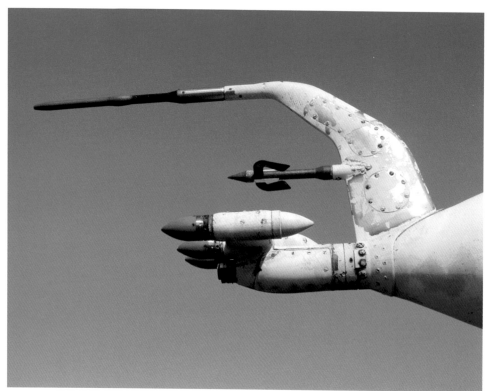

The «goose» of the Fencer-A/B/C – the characteristic L-shaped strut carrying the pitot, ILS aerial and ESM antennas.

Close-up of the antenna dishes of the Orion-A fire control radar and the Rel'yef terrain following radar below it forming the PNS-24 Tigr navigation/attack avionics suite. The antenns are mounted on a solid frame which swings out to starboard for access to the radar sets. The stencils on the antenna dishes read «Attention! Tuned, do not touch». Note also the V-shaped window of the TP-23E infra-red seeker.

The Su-24 features a sharply swept two-piece windshield made of strong polycarbonate. It is designed to minimise drag at high speed and withstand birdstrikes which are quite likely during low-level dashes. Note the PVD-7 pitot head in line with the windshield.

Boarding ladders are hooked up to the Su-24's cockpit sills.

The two halves on the canopy can be opened individually, leaving a splitter running down the middle. The construction number is normally stencilled on this (though not on this particular aircraft).

▲
Close-up of the faired centreline pylons carrying MBD3-U6-68 MERs.

▶
The Su-24 has a levered-suspension twin-wheel nose gear unit equipped with a mud/snow/slush guard to prevent engine damage on semi-prepared runways.

Close-up of the Chaika (Seagull) under-nose forward-looking infra-red seeker (FLIR)/laser ranger window and Filin (Horned owl) ESM antennas.
◀

The bold, tough levered-suspension main gear units are designed to cope with the worst thinkable runways and high ordnance loads.
▼

◄ The instrument panel of the Su-24 featured illuminated push-button switches; some of the engine instruments are of the vertical strip type. The diagram in the centre with the aircraft silhouette and radial beams is the RHAWS indicator.

Overall view of the cockpit. The navigator/weapons systems officer (WSO) sits on the right, detecting targets on the orange-coloured radar screen and the display above it. This aircraft is c/n 1215301 (note «12-01» stencilled in the WSO's footwell). ▼

Another view of the cockpit with its conventional electromechanical flight instruments. The throttles are on the captain's side console.

As the Su-24 can only land safely with the wings at minimum sweep, a read emergency wing actuating handle is located on the WSO's instrument panel to the left of the airspeed indicator.

The T6-1 as originally flown (minus downward-angled wingtips.

Aptly coded «62 Yellow», the T6-2I was the first variable-geometry prototype.

The T6-27 during weapons trials. The aircraft is a Fencer-B.

«40 White», a 149th Guards Fighter Regiment Su-24 Fencer-B which saw action in Afghanistan, operating out of Kokaidy, Uzbekistan. Note the 13 mission markers.

The T6-8M (the first prototype of the Su-24M) in ultimate configuration.

A production Su-24M in non-standard tactical camouflage.

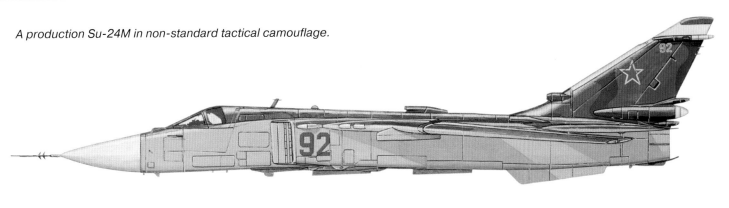

Another Su-24M in a highly unusual colour scheme applied in the early 1990s. Note the «eyes» painted on the forward fuselage for bird-scaring. The Russian flag addition to the red star was short-lived.

A Ukrainian Air Force Su-24MR. Note the old-style round tail insignia and the Guards badge.

An Iraqi Air Force (al Quwwat al-Jawwiya al-Iraqiya) Su-24MK serialled 24246.

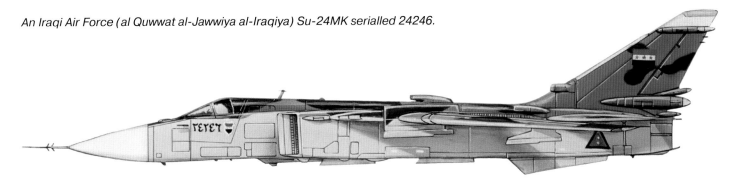

An Islamic Republic of Iran Air Force Su-24MK serialled 3-6808.

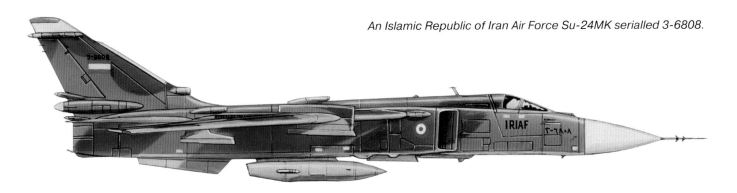

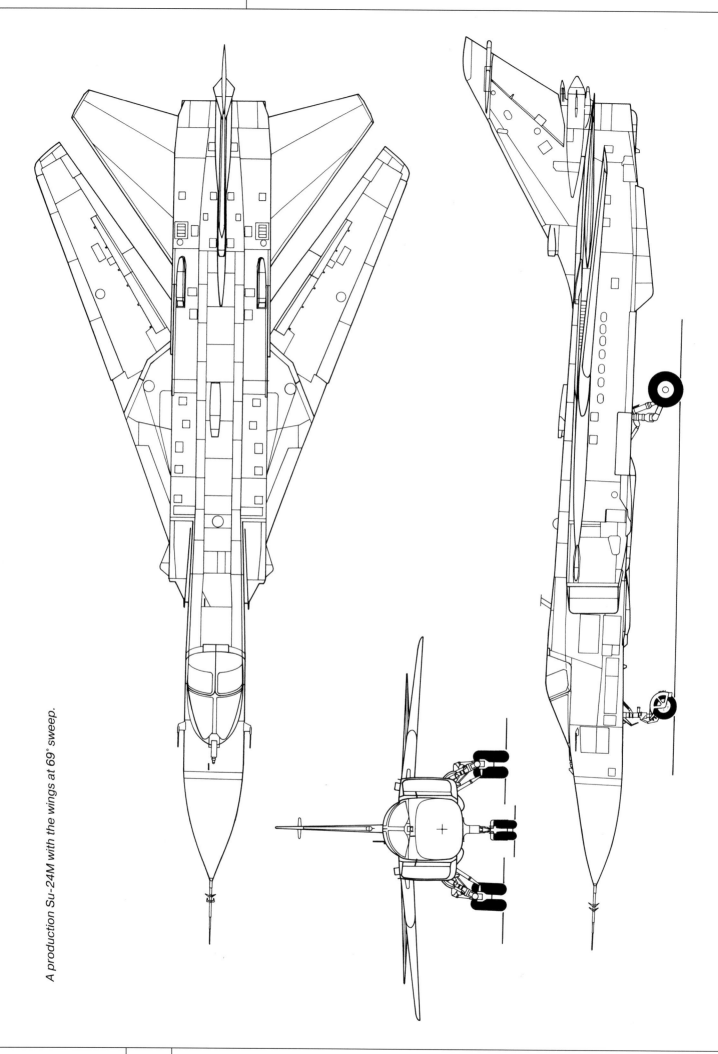

A production Su-24M with the wings at 69° sweep.